Product of our Environment

J. M. SALVIN

Copyright © 2021 J. M. Salvin

All rights reserved.

ISBN: 9798760042118

DEDICATION

For Danielle, Harry and Benji.
Love you lots x

CONTENTS

	Acknowledgments	i
A Drop of Consideration	Lineage and Loving Women	13
	Scarecrow Man	15
	Convalescence	16
	Inadequacy	18
	Contentment	20
	Perceived Likeness	21
	In the Silence	22
	A Need to be Heard	24
	The Longest Shift	25
	Performance	26
Culpability in Antagonism	A Benefit of Burden	28
	I didn't Forget	30
	Monsters in the Night	31
	Intention	32

	Admission for One	33
	Predator	34
	Rationality	36
	Without Remorse	37
An Adaptation to Consequence	The Chaos of Nature	39
	Without Prediction	40
	Another Thursday	42
	Integrity	43
	Into Oblivion	44
	On my Sleeve	46
	Pretty Lies	47
	At Arm's Length	48
Chronicles of Lost Potential	Acknowledgement	51
	Disappointment	52
	Solstice	54
	Milestones	55
	4am	56

Product of Our Environment

	Wonky Little Sandcastles	57
Ignorance in Awareness	I am You	60
	Superstition	62
	Pitied Exploitation	64
	All of Nothing	66
	Grief	67
	On Monday	68
	Earning Indifference	69
	In the Maybes	71
Dead Men Tell Tall Tales	Children of Gaea	73
	Regretfully Alexander	75
	Temperance and Kakia	76
	Glory in Odysseus	77
	Hyacinth and Apollo	78
	Proteus as One	79
	Hephaestus in Detachment	80
	Persephone's Spring	81

Product of Our Environment

ACKNOWLEDGMENTS

With special thanks to my Mum, Helen, who has been my biggest support and best friend. Shoutout to Steph and Louise for encouraging me in my procrastination projects, my Dad for getting me interested in writing in the first place, and everyone else who's helped along the way. Love you all.

A DROP OF CONSIDERATION

Lineage and Loving Women

The lowest branch is snapped so easily

That it is assumed careless,

But she stands for seasons before,

And it was always when the leaves fell on her shoulders

That she knew it would stunt growth.

She has seen stumps in this forest

With many rings from many decades.

She has heard the disappointment from strangers.

What a waste, she is told, it had a greater purpose

Theft, she is told, results in ostracism.

When she breaks the branch she shows everyone she knows,

They will not understand she holds secret shame.

She anticipates the divulgence of thoughts they whisper out of earshot.

We will always be discussed in concerned tones

To reel out righteousness and indignation.

She doesn't know yet that her branch will grow a family tree of her own,

And she is braver for it.

Scarecrow Man

An extension of ourselves does not fall organically,

it is manufactured with guidance and caution,

and movement to care beyond himself is an emergence

of years to unravel into a familiar path.

If he is heard speaking quietly into empty beds of soil,

remember there is no rejection in the care for those who cannot respond,

and there is no abandonment in the certainty of compassionate development,

for there will always be hospice in calloused fingers.

The protection of few does not shelter maturation,

but the hardship of the rain is no longer feared,

and come winter he will not dwell on fallen leaves.

J. M. SALVIN

Convalescence

The direction to break apart an understanding of the world is not given linearly.

In the silent moments of fragmentation,

insight will often catch her by the jaw,

and the powerful grasp of the unknown does not evade her by its fleeting nature.

Trained aversion to a watchful eye that exists only in the fear of the faithful,

to be left shrouded in the discovery of others,

negligence will act as instruction,

and in the sweep of forgiving the lost she could cherish the found.

When tree roots explore the depths of forgotten dirt it is with purpose,

and when she established her standing it was not with certainty but need.

Although there are wooden pillars planted firmly in the ground, they remain untouched.

Her body was not reconstructed from vines,

she fought for her place in the forest,

and when flowers blossomed in her open palms

they reflected the sunlight she'd been harvesting for a brighter beginning.

She understands now what it means to be whole.

J. M. SALVIN

Inadequacy

She does not find it particularly charming

That you cannot wash your plate correctly.

Nor does she laugh fondly

When you hold your baby at arms length.

She will not smile

At the colour stained sheets

Or the charred countertop.

She used to think it was a sign of neglect

Until she met your sister,

Who met her gaze with same tiredness.

Your mother did her job perfectly,

Exactly the way she was told,

But full stomachs and clean underwear does not create consideration.

She will never find gentle humour

In the knowledge her future had been taught.

She has become a replacement,

And one day will be left at the doorstep

For a doe eyed child with expectations of love.

Contentment

If you lure him to the edge of the village

His foot will not pass the border.

In a bastardisation of his stance

He is known to be stubborn,

But he is not lost.

With fingers on his pulse and eyes on his grave,

He is not baited by succession,

And in the mouths of his brothers

His children will live in acceptance.

You do not have to view him as aspirational,

He does not need to be,

A man who lives in the contentment of his home

Learns little from his travels.

Perceived Likeness

A stab in the dark makes contact with nothingness

And relief will always flood my body

I do not know,

Are we entitled to happiness,

Or do we have to earn it?

Will I be looked down at with fondness, or disgust?

One final act,

as a human with no space for encore,

Is there room to breathe in those shallow lungs?

Do you feel yourself becoming enclosed,

Like me?

Do I remind you of what you could become,

Or are our similarities imagined?

I wish better for you.

J. M. SALVIN

In the Silence

He would hate for me to call him gentle

Or refer to him at all,

And I am not here to criticise his open wounds.

He does not see me as a concern,

The men who see the unloveable as maternal

Do not view me as a threat.

He knows I will not mock him

Or discuss his shortcomings with baited breath.

I will accept him, as everyone else would have,

But with me he knows for sure.

And I am aware, I always was.

We are creating a pattern of fearing the secure

And averting eyes from their crowds,

Only to provide consul when they are left behind.

One day, if I accidentally mention your names,

I hope you're not too embarrassed.

I have still kept your secrets.

A Need to be Heard

Closing your mouth

Does not define you as silent.

If I was asked to stake capital

On the girl who would grow to be heard,

I would choose your moment of hesitation

Rooted in kindness,

And know soon there will be no lead to follow.

Your strides now are longer than mine

And I let you run with open arms.

The Longest Shift

I see the child in her every day now,

It kicks and screams for fairness,

And demands to be heard.

When I see her met with underwhelming reactions I am reminded

That breaking this loop is not only difficult for myself.

I want to be unaware,

But it would mean losing us and what we have become together.

I need your adoration, it's not believable from anyone else,

And one day, when child is all that you are,

I will fulfil the role you've always wanted

And you will be at peace.

Performance

They seem to be rehearsing for plays,

They mimic and adjust into something more cohesive.

When the violence is folded into passiveness,

They don't understand why I ask if they feel seen.

Of course, they say,

We have had audience since dawn.

CULPABILITY IN ANTAGONISM

J. M. SALVIN

A Benefit of Burden

I feel unease in this stance,

there is no shelter in the light of judgement.

Self-assurance and stagnancy peel my fingers from the ledge,

And I am dropped feet first into dark waters.

I can see nothing,

only the air that leaves my mouth,

And I follow those bubbles towards the surface

To allow my caged lungs to expand.

It smells rotten,

to kick frantically in the open jaw of desecration.

Eyes up, ears open, the bound body is held entombed

In the wake of men and their suffering.

I taste wickedness,

The status of war is not always spoken to our kind,

And when I clamp down on the flesh of my tongue I am secure,

By definition a dictation of endurance.

I listen only to his name,

He does not reply in kindness, but sincere retribution.

My need to become melded with those I cannot hear is dismissed.

We are not held together by string.

I Didn't Forget.

You are watched.

We like to say never in the sinister sense,

But far too often you are held gently between our teeth

In an effort to confirm the bitter taste we fear from your fallings.

Tell them what you meant last winter,

Explain your misfortune,

And hold yourself to those words.

I know you would understand,

But how can I convince entitlement to give a little more?

Why, when the dulcet tones remind me of your apology?

Your guilt is etched into my palms,

So, tell me it no longer crosses your mind.

Monsters in the Night

It cracking joints and dirty nails and it is a person

Not an it, a he.

He is not a monstrous anomaly.

I saw his soul retract into sullen eyes, but he did not become inhuman.

The fingers that dug their way into my neck held a wedding band, they were not born in evil.

If my head connects with hardened plastic a fourth time I do not feel it,

And although this happens in churches and classrooms and kitchens,

I thought my impurities would keep me safe.

I am ugly. It is ugly. He is ugly.

We are both human,

And that does not deserve the praise it's given.

Intention

A world which burns brighter in revelation

Cannot bear the thoughts of unkindness to follow.

Their teeth rot inside sweetened skulls,

Richness does not heed warning.

How else would he become blessed?

Does he leave me isolated with purpose?

When we rowed into darkness that night only one of us returned.

Although your guilt does not stem from partition,

I am held in the knowledge that you cannot seek forgiveness

For an act you do not regret.

The wages of the wretched come with bleeding soles,

I am sworn, as one,

To be held witness to our refractory nature.

Admission for One

A word that holds so little meaning to him

Tore through the pillars he'd reconstructed with paper.

What's one word to a fragile man

Who cannot stay silent?

What's a confession in a crowd of strangers

Who's fleeting attention gave no relief?

He removed my guilt with his understanding,

And though he does not deserve peace,

I feel I owe him the same.

It mattered to me.

Predator

I can to tell you a story

That you will not believe.

I would like to be returned into darkness,

I can only be forgiven when I am blind,

But the actions of the wary is cowardice.

The wings of a demon have been folded,

And the faith of his shaking hands gave him resonance.

That's not possible, I told him that is not possible,

But I am shaken once more into acknowledgement.

He offers himself in a servitude I cannot bring myself to love,

There is meaning in wilful ignorance.

I feel no acceptance in his lack of change,

My skin will take years to heal.

I encounter peaceful silence when my words are feared,

And he receives the encouragement and imagination gifted to children.

There is no remembrance in this shallow ground,

I will never know if he sins in my name.

Product of Our Environment

Without Remorse

Fear the man

Who never addressed his guilt in the dead of night,

Who did not wonder how it would feel to be clean,

Who let his chest expand without restriction in the face of his actions.

Tell me a fable

Of those who allow us to reconsider,

who plant seeds they don't return to,

And accept our imperfections in sunlight.

AN ADAPTATION TO CONSEQUENCE

The Chaos of Nature

Harbours crumble to the will of her ocean

and as our presence closes to none,

she grows.

Our view felt important,

yet she extends regardless

and the wreckage of our progression is swallowed whole.

When she becomes Mother again she will not discriminate,

she will provide.

And forgotten,

A charlatan's justification falls on deaf ears,

harm and chaos lies only

in the souls of those who could not pass.

Without Prediction

She has been unsettled in the knowledge we have spoken.

The thought had not occurred to her,

That one day we would both slip from her grasp so easily.

Although her knuckles are still white,

Our weight has been long since removed.

Self-proclaimed wisdom from the narcissist without insight,

How are we reflected in her anger?

Are we to speak over mushroom clouds at the dinner table,

Or in the watchful silence of travels home?

I have lost my trust,

It has become hard to decipher in the monologues of the selfish.

Have we now infiltrated poisoned words?

When I see her falter, is she seeking my awareness?

Does she know?

J. M. SALVIN

Another Thursday

Press your shoe into my neck,

I will not swallow.

I can pluck every petal from that plastic rose,

And it still won't dissolve in the water.

You have torn apart what it meant to be human,

And on someone prettier,

This may have been an easier sight to endure

Or understand.

I was already in the depths,

Do you care that drove me further into the river?

Did you feel remorse sewing rocks to my clothes?

Do you even remember?

Integrity

We are built from allowance,

But I cannot test virtue with your gaze.

I am not held by my convictions,

They squirm through my fingertips

And shrivel on the ground.

I may be kind without the feeling of your presence,

But now I will never know for sure.

I don't know how to break apart my intentions,

And although I feel them with sincerity,

Doubt has always been sown to my actions.

I would like to be good,

But I fear I don't know how.

J. M. SALVIN

Into Oblivion

Under-correction excludes the steady path

On which travellers find themselves trailing after a sun that will never set.

When vultures circle above the children will watch in awe,

and remark how perfect their summers have become.

The horizon will be enjoyed in spite of its warnings of despair,

and reciprocates in abundance with an anticipated release.

A poisonous exhale,

Which will not be held in the ribcages of greedy,

But the needy.

Even so,

feigned ignorance lined the pockets of those in their wake,

who wonder why consideration was not allocated beyond their caskets.

They burn together.

J. M. SALVIN

On my Sleeve

I have been too hasty,

I hope you forgive me.

I have fallen in love

With a woman you have never known,

And when I left you behind,

I never gave a thought to the people I left you with.

I had forgotten the way she curled

And twisted until you lost breath.

I had forgotten the way she gripped tight,

And ripped you from what could have been.

I hope you don't grow to resent me,

But I hope more that you never understand,

Because what would truth do for us now,

Other than erode the final strings of belonging?

Pretty Lies

Adrenaline has worn off and I cannot bleed.

Your artificial burning brings me no heat,

Although I can watch with disdain when you are fawned over.

It is late enough for confession now, I promise.

No one will hear.

You have stolen power,

It only knows bounds in your hands.

Forgive me, my legs tire easily,

And you walk five paces ahead.

You were my favourite.

At Arm's Length

I watch their eyes around her,

In times they fall near I know my pulse will betray us,

then deafen the normality of the day.

They will become Him.

And, although I was told to stay calm in crisis,

I would never have been much of a leader anyway.

One day I will notice an innocent look from a man I love,

But when you don't run from a hungry tiger it takes thought,

And courage,

And dedication.

If one day I stop observing and she slips through the cracks,

Where would we fall?

I have no desire watch myself reconstructed in her body,

And reflect what we have always feared,

That no amount of care will divert blood.

I fear path is also chosen.

J. M. SALVIN

CHRONICLES OF LOST POTENTIAL

Acknowledgement

I know you find comfort in my chaos,

that is how my company is defined.

I wonder if you see me for my incompetence,

Or if you wait for me to return.

I don't know whether I am this failing,

Or the one before it.

I hope you never know what it's like to look up to normalcy,

And beg not fall further.

This is no longer a temporary state,

It is my being.

I have become my worst nightmare,

And I am lied to, to feel okay.

I am not who I could have been,

And only a few miles in,

Everyone else has passed the finish line.

Disappointment

The things I said too quietly implicate this denial,

I do not know why I lowered myself with gratitude,

Or accepted these pins in my spine,

But I cannot address my part in this destruction.

When we are to fall together,

I will not tug your wings into place.

They will be torn, ripped apart.

My place beside you will be taken as punishment,

Not indulgence.

It is not the gift you presented,

It is the soil you push me into.

The blood smells sour, it has begun to rot in my veins,

I hope it poisons your hunger and leaves you scarred.

You said you would remove this,

You told me it would be simpler.

Weathered wood is not as strong as you promised.

Solstice

I can understand now,

Why people grow wary over Christmas songs in November.

It's not a disregard for happiness,

It's another year that has slipped through my fingers.

I am biding my time,

But tomorrow it will be March,

And I have barely adjusted to the cold.

How long have I spent here?

Rationality

Only with his fingers in my throat

Can I taste the bitterness of his anger,

And when I search for his soul I'm faced with more canvases.

He is reflected in dreams, not nightmares,

Where he blends into normality.

And, if he slips into memory when I pour my coffee,

Who am I to let him be burned?

Milestones

Achievements restated hurt less over time.

But, when I watch the forced smile from the picture of health,

reassurances solidify as lies

and I falter.

I hold judgement, too,

derangement is only blocked by my tongue.

I do not fumble my feelings anymore,

but I cannot feel the the compulsion

To justify what hasn't lived.

There is no letting, they move through instinct.

When I strive for mediocrity I will keep my envy silent,

But I will not hide joy when my feet plant firmly on the stepping stones along the way.

4am

When it falls midnight he curls beneath the comfortable silence,

No ray of responsibility will fall through windowsill in his next exhale.

A radiator saves heat for the working,

And the quiet snores above serve to remind him

Chasing these moments will never become less of an exercise.

How many peaceful hours repair the potential of the man who let go?

How many destroyed it?

Product of Our Environment

Wonky Little Sandcastles

I'll admit it was a little rough

To watch the grains dissolve through cold fingers.

Once in a while we have to understand

That hard work doesn't always come with praise.

The temperance of a liar is seen through their smiles,

And one by one when they do not glance behind

I come to learn of the bitterness I wanted to compete with.

Sometimes, in the lull of the morning,

I make my commitment to avoidance.

It does not feel concrete,

But over time,

Days,

    Weeks,

        Months,

A decision becomes a habit,

And a habit becomes a trait.

In our behaviour we shape our description.

If not the perception of our loved ones, who are we?

And if I left,

If this is how I remain,

Addiction shrouded beneath its deception

Or worse,

A scorned child never adjusted,

What was the point?

IGNORANCE IN AWARENESS

J. M. SALVIN

I am You

Earthside I explore moons to find my sister,

There are plenty here planted in my blood.

I am lonely.

Wilted frames to not crumble in my tight grasp,

I worry I will never escape this cycle.

Give my the presence I beg for,

Let me know you are looking, too.

I am not asking for connection,

Just let this narcissism die at my feet.

We can live in separate houses,

You can take our friends and children,

Just let me know your sight is not born in mine.

Do not allow this death to transform again,

I am tired of meeting myself.

I know this destruction is mine,

But in this body I cannot change her path.

I have let my hatred grow beyond self-destruction,

You will be injured from my lack of control.

Allow me intervention,

I will not stop this harm until you tie my hands.

I will not become good.

You have given me years,

I continue to shred the wood chips.

Plant these trees again,

they deserve more.

I am sorry,

but not enough.

Superstition

I wonder if the moon knows

That when I call her beautiful I am going to ask another favour.

It does not change that I am telling the truth.

I touch branches and hope she will hear my wishes.

I salute to birds, and tap my cigarettes,

I do not step on cracks or drains,

And nothing changes.

A one-sided dependency is not born in love, but desperation.

When we are alone I feel her warmth.

I do not feel seen,

I do not feel heard,

I do not feel loved.

I thank her for that, and dread to imagine what I would have become

If she had served me acceptance in my darkest of times.

When the sun rises, he will tell me of my squandered youth.

He will tell me it is not patience, or betterment.

He will let me know that the warmth I feel in her presence

Is simply his borrowed light.

We cannot remain burrowed,

For we will continue to dig,

And our placeholder will not be a painting.

I will continue, in fear of a downward swing.

Perhaps this abandonment

Is another I will seek.

J. M. SALVIN

Pitied Exploitation

To think I threw it all away

For some bread and butter.

When I swallow my nature,

And kneel beside the door,

I have to wonder if there was a chance.

I was never looking for better odds

But I consulted above.

One sided, of course,

And returned empty handed.

They told me once

That in the entitlement of man

The question yearned is comedy enough.

Purpose is not granted,

But it would not exist without curiosity.

Greed and growth intertwine,

hand in hand.

Our meaning comes from exploration,

from this need we expand.

We have come too far to fall behind,

East of the branches our exploits lie unsheltered.

Queasy, once more, how could we have gorged again

at the expense of free roaming cruelty?

Admonishment is held in the palms of the self righteous,

in a pretty disguise for those who wouldn't have noticed.

I have dressed up victimhood for the last time.

J. M. SALVIN

All of Nothing

I do not understand proportionality.

If I feel cash in my wallet I will stretch it open

And shake out the coins until I hear the last penny clink on the ground.

Powder is finished before the night has started,

I do not save the chocolate for later,

And my final week is extended by a day or two.

I am given praise or burning hatred,

They look at me with admiration or not at all,

And I am supported or sabotaged.

My soul is redirected for another day.

I am still here.

I am still here?

I am still here.

So what now?

Grief

And when brittle bones cracked between our fingers we said nothing,

October fell and we did not celebrate another cycle.

Certainty crumbled in the wake of confidence

And we paused to bask in the discomfort of youth.

One by one

We loosen our grasp of the fraying thread,

And when betrayal creeps into our conscience

We pray.

On Monday

There is no reason in this acceptance,

I am not held by my achievements.

If this is an unfair metric to hold,

Why can everyone else do it?

I am perfect until I am greedy,

I am controlled until I undo this collar.

Lie to me, tell me this is okay,

Tell me I will not die with my fingers down my throat.

I am not striving for perfection,

I am praying for normality.

I would like to be unrecognisable,

I would like to start over,

So I will.

And again.

And again.

Unchanged.

Earning Indifference

I have lived in discomfort for so long,

I would not know what it meant to feel at ease.

But,

when my sister embraces me before she leaves for school,

and when she comes home,

and when she asks a question,

and when she wants to tell me something,

and when she is bored,

and when she is happy,

and when she is sad,

and before she falls asleep,

and then once more,

for good luck,

I understand the dismay when her normalcy wants to change shape, and in that comfort only then do I learn to accept my body

for what it is,

warm.

In the Maybes

If you were to throw a matchstick into fire I would not notice,

But I would care if you spit on the shore.

When sweat sticks to compulsion we see our reflection,

And the harmony of what once was bores into bruised hands.

The flames have dwindled.

And one day, when even the ash has blown away,

I will remember your drop in the ocean and falter again.

DEAD MEN TELL TALL TALES

Children of Gaea

An unwelcoming embrace of antagonism

means the familial is left in the hands of the angered,

and once in a blue moon when I avert my eyes

I am faced with what it means to be forgotten.

After years of begging you to change,

I thought envy would fall at my feet when I saw your gentle hands push him forward,

and whisper silent encouragements from behind.

I thought your compassion had been removed before our time,

but now I know your defiance was for my actions all.

Your biology has become shameless violence and I do not care to tug on its sleeve.

Once the scratched paint peels away,

will your shaking hand be there to collect it?

Would your allowance have an effect on a weathered mind,

Or in the end are we left behind?

Worse still,

Ignored?

Regretfully Alexander

His care is not impulsive anymore,

It feels heavy in his bones,

And is etched into every interaction.

He is heard at dawn

With his fingernails dragging cement,

And his voice in his throat.

He does not feel owed, nor owned.

Outreach is a state of isolation and he bleeds all the same.

This time there will be no hysteria in his love.

No ill-timed compassion,

And still,

Only one is left to hear.

She is enough,

On the good days.

J. M. SALVIN

Temperance and Kakia

Your abstinence is not commendable,

And she is not foolish in expending your means.

The divorce from instinct,

Striving to a perfection that will flee,

Is not the fruits of your labour.

Exchange your good will for pleasure,

Lower yourself to harmony

In the knowledge there is little judgment

In the arms of the hedonistic.

She may not strike you to damnation,

But she will cast doubt in your heart,

And devolve the righteousness of purity.

She is the will of your subconscious

To unhinge your jaw and accept her desire.

Temptation smells sweet to the man living in vain.

Glory in Odysseus

The direct outcome of a summer afternoon,

If I cover my bases,

does not topple my house of cards.

I braid love into her hair,

I rest my chin on her shoulder.

I watch her work

in spirit

as she weaves me into existence.

I pretend not to notice

when she peels drying clay from her fingers,

or leaves her loom on the edge of the dresser.

She would like to feel pride, and it is when I see her most human.

She is devotion, even in doubt.

J. M. SALVIN

Hyacinth and Apollo

I parted clouds to view you easier in this sunlight,

I should have known.

The west winds slow in admiration,

I should have known.

Providence and discretion mean nothing now,

I should have known.

I cannot heal you from fate,

I should have known.

I should have known.

I should have known.

You weigh nothing in my arms,

And in returning you to the earth I am not burdened less.

I created a flower in your name,

Its beauty holds my grief.

Product of Our Environment

Proteus as one

We are employed by the actions of saviours.

We operate under the responsibility of agency.

I do not crave contagion,

but to know capability.

I am faced yet with navigation,

I am held selfishly in dishonest memorandum.

I cannot fathom what it has meant for you

To empathise with apprehensive need.

I do not want advocacy,

This motion is not a yearning to be understood.

My quarrel was never with connection.

My bribery is not glanced at,

And I feel silly but not forsaken in this neglect.

When we are rejected I know my name,

And I will not belittle your evasiveness.

J. M. SALVIN

Hephaestus in Detachment

Do you believe we are born free?

We cannot be destined indenture.

Utility is not an injunction, assistance in faith is kind.

The valley of doubt wells above my need.

Damnation is not a price too steep,

For the little insight bred in our bones

Do not wish to be interpreted.

Reconcile with their misconceptions.

How do you break a connection

Without fraying the ends?

Can I burn rope until it is sealed and charred?

Or do I pull it thread by thread?

Be my marred skin in this view, hold your voice as your own.

Deprive us of pressure.

Persephone's Spring

This house feels old and frayed.

she opens her mouth to describe her love,

Yet there is rust in her gums.

In parables she is made to feel trodden.

A fireplace belongs in the heart of the home,

But she feels his warmth closest to the kitchen.

In those precious seconds,

His hands would ghost the window ledge,

And she would embrace his being.

How does he want her to feel light when he has ripped out the bulb?

Does he expect her to compress his smile,

And bask in the sun?

Printed in Great Britain
by Amazon